T0046325

Pre-reader
Dive, Dolphin!
Shira Evans
NATIONAL GEOGRAPHIC
Washington, D.C.

Vocabulary Tree

DOLPHINS

WHERE THEY LIVE	WHAT THEY DO	WHAT THEY HAVE
ocean	dive	flipper
river	swim	fin
	hunt	tail
	play	
	leap	
	jump	
	breathe	

Dive, dolphin!

There are many kinds of dolphins.
Some have long beaks.

Some have short beaks.

These dolphins have stripes.

This dolphin has spots.

Some dolphins live in oceans.

Others live in rivers.

fin
tail

All dolphins have flippers, a fin, and a tail.

Dolphins swim together.

They work as a team to hunt fish.

Dolphins like to play with things they find in the water.

This dolphin plays with seaweed.

They also like to leap and jump.

Dolphins need to breathe.

They come to the top of the water to get air.

Dive, dolphin!

Dolphin Habitat Map

Dolphins live in oceans and rivers around the world. Here's where these dolphins live.

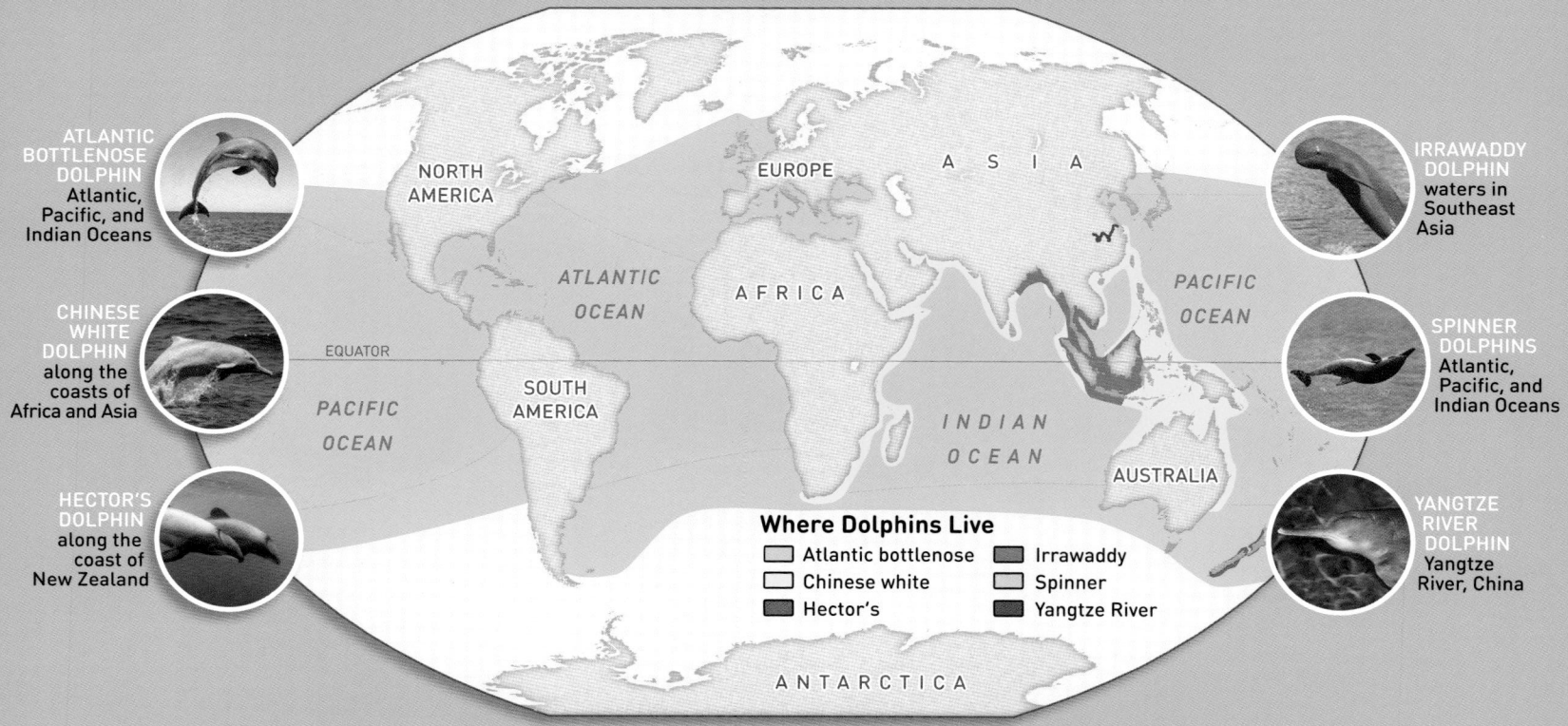

YOUR TURN!

Match the word to the photo. Use your finger to make a line from the word to the photo.

PLAY

JUMP

HUNT

BREATHE

The answer is on the next page.

Published by National Geographic Partners, LLC, Washington, DC 20036.

Copyright © 2016 National Geographic Partners, LLC. All rights reserved. Reproduction in whole or in part without written permission of the publisher is prohibited.

NATIONAL GEOGRAPHIC and Yellow Border Design are trademarks of the National Geographic Society, used under license.

The publisher gratefully acknowledges the expert literacy review of this book by Susan B. Neuman, Ph.D., professor of early childhood and literacy education, New York University.

Designed by Rachel Kenny

Library of Congress Cataloging-in-Publication Data

Names: Evans, Shira, author. | National Geographic Society (U.S.)
Title: Dive, dolphin! / by Shira Evans.
Description: 1st edition. | Washington, DC : National Geographic Partners, 2016. | Series: National geographic readers | Audience: Ages 2-5.
Identifiers: LCCN 2016005543| ISBN 9781426324406 (pbk. : alk. paper) | ISBN 9781426324413 (library binding : alk. paper)
Subjects: LCSH: Dolphins--Juvenile literature.
Classification: LCC QL737.C432 E93 2016 | DDC 599.53--dc23
LC record available at https://lccn.loc.gov/2016005543

Photo Credits
Cover, Brandon Cole; 1, Willyam Bradberry/Shutterstock; 2-3, Hiroya Minakuchi/Minden Pictures; 4, Mark Carwardine/Minden Pictures; 5, Greg Boreham/TrekLightly/Getty Images; 6, Brandon Cole/Kimball Stock; 7, Jim Abernethy/Getty Images; 8, Doug Perrine/Blue Planet Archive; 9, Kevin Schafer/Minden Pictures; 10-11, Jeff Rotman/Getty Images; 12, Alexander Safonov/Getty Images; 14-15, Reinhard Dirscherl/Minden Pictures; 16-17, Stuart Westmorland/Getty Images; 18-19, Flip Nicklin/Minden Pictures; 20-21, Juergen and Christine Sohns/Getty Images; 22 (UP LE), Roland Seitre/Nature Picture Library; 22 (UP CTR), Flip Nicklin/Minden Pictures; 22 (UP RT), Roland Seitre/Minden Pictures; 22 (LO LE), Mike Hill/Getty Images; 22 (LO CTR), Thomas Jefferson/Blue Planet Archive; 22 (LO RT), Tobias Bernhard Raff/Minden Pictures; 23 (UP), Stuart Westmorland/Getty Images; 23 (CTR UP), Flip Nicklin/Minden Pictures; 23 (CTR LO), Reinhard Dirscherl/Minden Pictures; 23 (LO), Alexander Safonov/Getty Images; 24 (UP), Jeff Rotman/Getty Images; 24 (LO, A), Stuart Westmorland/Getty Images; 24 (LO, B), Flip Nicklin/Minden Pictures; 24 (LO, C), Reinhard Dirscherl/Minden Pictures; 24 (LO, D), Alexander Safonov/Getty Images

Printed in the United States of America
22/WOR/2

ANSWER:

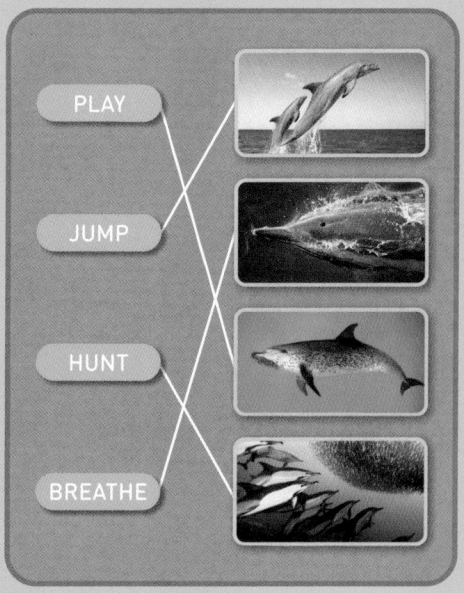